SEAN MOSES IS
MARTIN LUTHER,
THE KING *Jr.*

SEAN MOSES IS
MARTIN LUTHER, THE KING Jr.

MOSES D. POWE

Illustrated by Angelina Valieva

FATHERLESS
FATHERS PUBLISHING
A POWEM PUBLISHERS IMPRINT

Sean Moses is Martin Luther, The King Jr.

Fatherless Fathers Publishing (A POWEM PUBLISHERS IMPRINT)
1603 Capitol Avenue, Suite 310 A145
Cheyenne, Wyoming 82001
www.mosespowe.com

ISBN (hardcover): 9781735180335
ISBN (paperback): 9781735180342
eISBN: 9781735180359

Library of Congress Control Number: 2020950045

MEMORY WALL

This book is dedicated to the memory of the young kings and queens who will never get to see their dreams become a reality.

Isaiah Lewis~Antwon Rose~Jordan Edwards~David Joseph~Maurice S. Gordon~Shaun Lee Fuhr~Breonna Taylor~Barry Gedeus~Jaquyn Light~Michael Dean~Atatiana Jefferson~Jimmy Atchison~Danny Washington~Jacob Servais~Charles Roundtree~James Leatherwood~ Marcus-David L. Peters~Juan Jones~Stephon Clark~Cameron Hall~ Darion Baker~Michael Wilson~Calvin Toney~Anthony Ford~Isaiah Tucker~Dejuan Guillory~Ricco Holden~ Alteria Woods~Raynard Burton~Chad Robertson~Darrion Barnhill~Levonia Riggins~Donnell Thompson~Dalvin Hollins~Deravis Rogers~Vernell Bing~Michael Wilson~Jessica Nelson-Williams~Christopher Davis~Dyzhawn Perkins~Calin Roquemore~Keith Childress~Nathaniel Pickett~ Jamar Clark~Anthony Ashford~Keith McLeod~India Kager~ Christian Taylor~Albert Davis~Darrius Stewart~Victor Larosa~Kris Jackson~Brendo Glenn~David Felix~William Chapman~Brandon Jones~Anthony Hill~Tony Robinson~Lavall Hall~Jeremy Lett

source: Washington Post database

"Injustice anywhere is a threat to justice everywhere."

Reverend Doctor Martin Luther King Jr.

January 15, 1929 - April 4, 1968

Sean Moses could not wait to get home from school.
He wanted to share some wonderful news with his parents.

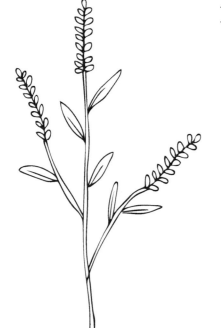

After the school bus dropped him off at his stop, he ran into the house with sonic speed.

"DAD! MOM! Guess what? Guess what?"

His mother was startled. She thought something was wrong.

His father asked, "Son, what's going on?"

Sean Moses paused for a moment to catch his breath. His parents anxiously waited to hear what he would say next.

"My teacher asked me to speak at the Black History Month program next week. You are not going to believe which Black leader I have to portray."

6

"Who?" his parents asked in unison.

"Before I tell you, you both have to guess one person."

His father decided to guess first. "Son, I believe you're going to be Malcolm X."

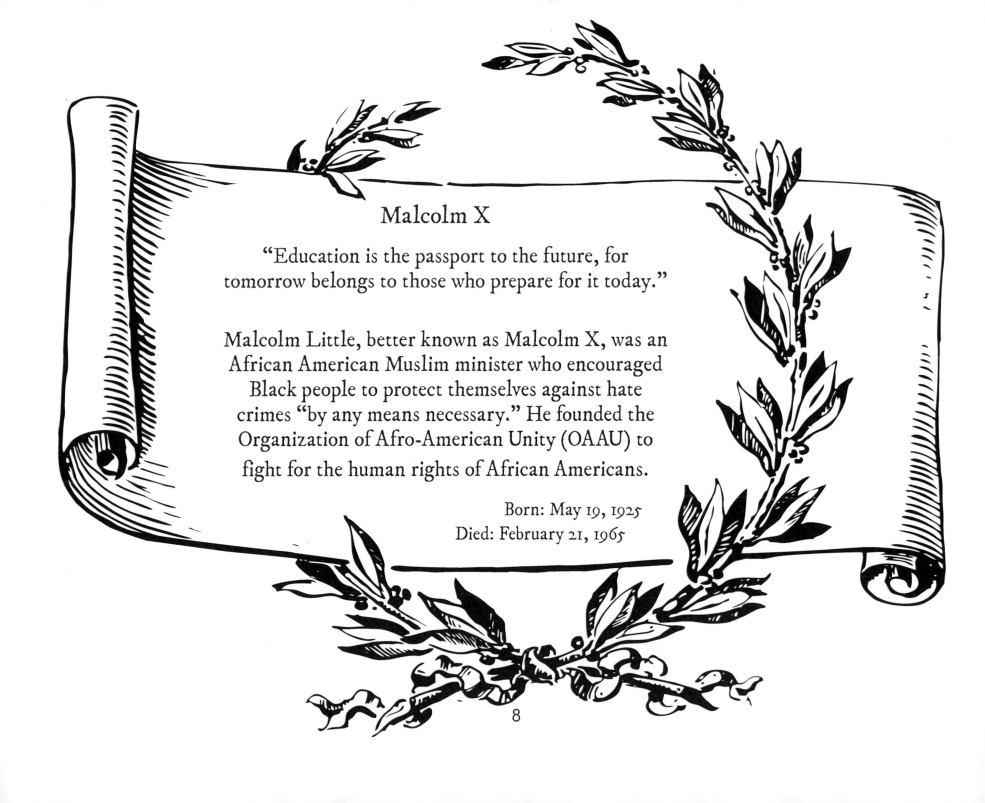

Malcolm X

"Education is the passport to the future, for tomorrow belongs to those who prepare for it today."

Malcolm Little, better known as Malcolm X, was an African American Muslim minister who encouraged Black people to protect themselves against hate crimes "by any means necessary." He founded the Organization of Afro-American Unity (OAAU) to fight for the human rights of African Americans.

Born: May 19, 1925
Died: February 21, 1965

"Dad, you are incorrect. Mom, who do you think?"

"Hmmm, let me see . . . Could it be Frederick Douglass, W.E.B. Du Bois, or Marcus Garvey?"

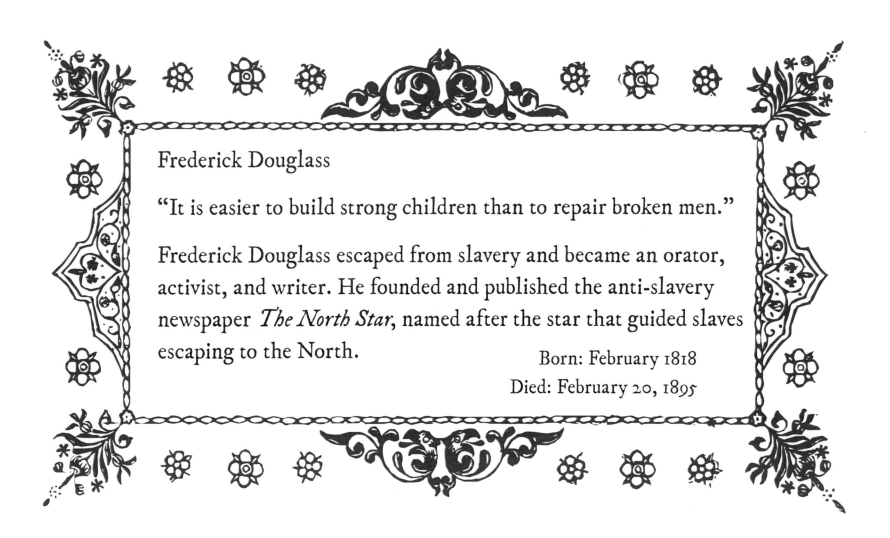

Frederick Douglass

"It is easier to build strong children than to repair broken men."

Frederick Douglass escaped from slavery and became an orator, activist, and writer. He founded and published the anti-slavery newspaper *The North Star*, named after the star that guided slaves escaping to the North.

Born: February 1818
Died: February 20, 1895

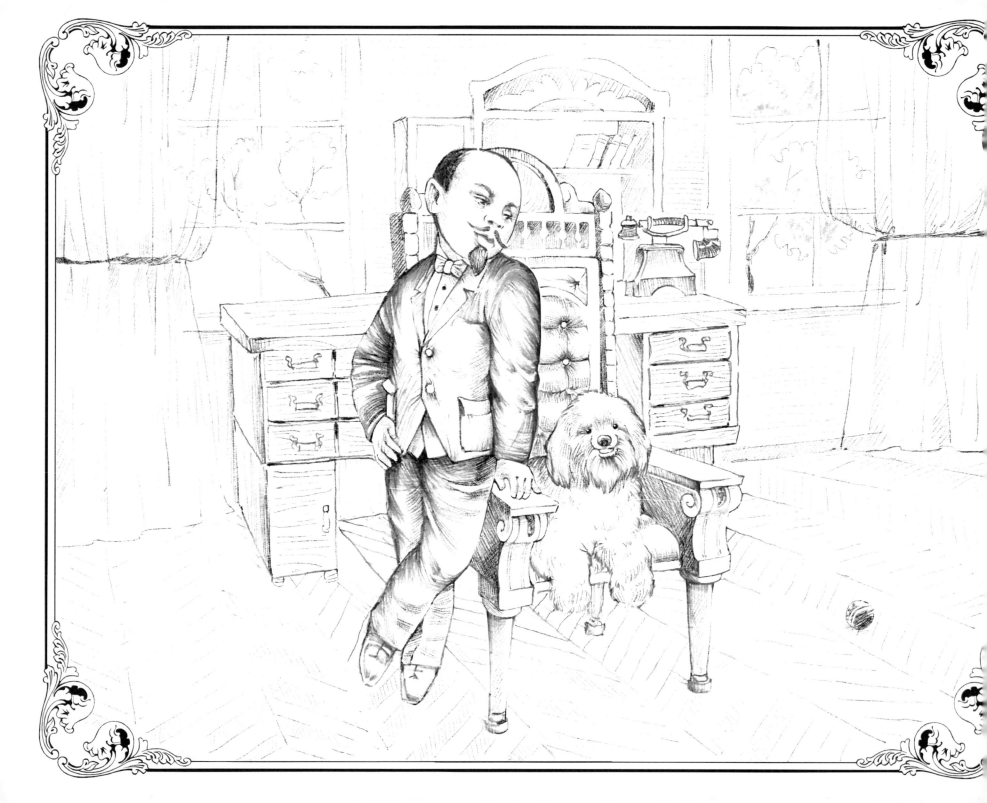

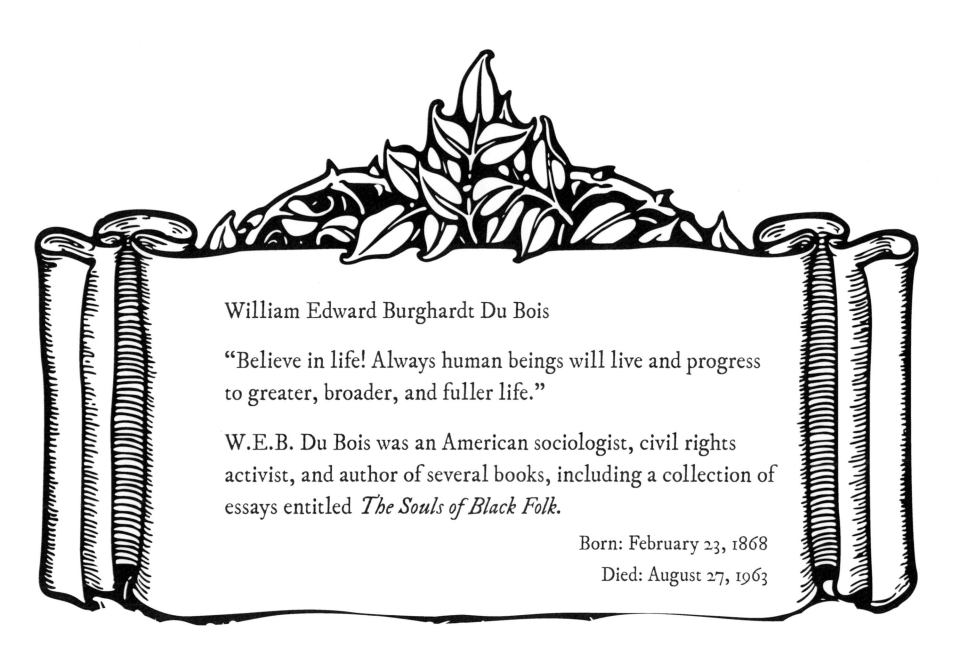

William Edward Burghardt Du Bois

"Believe in life! Always human beings will live and progress to greater, broader, and fuller life."

W.E.B. Du Bois was an American sociologist, civil rights activist, and author of several books, including a collection of essays entitled *The Souls of Black Folk.*

Born: February 23, 1868
Died: August 27, 1963

Marcus Mosiah Garvey, Sr.

"A people without the knowledge of their past history, origin and culture is like a tree without roots."

Marcus Garvey was a Jamaican-born political activist who founded the Universal Negro Improvement Association (UNIA). He's credited with coining the phrase "Black is beautiful."

Born: August 17, 1887
Died: June 10, 1940

"Mom, that was three guesses! And none of them are right."

His father chimed in, "Maybe you will portray Thurgood Marshall or Sergeant William Carney?"

The Honorable
Thurgood Marshall

"In recognizing the humanity of our fellow beings, we pay ourselves the highest tribute."

Thurgood Marshall, a graduate of the Howard University School of Law, helped end segregation in public schools. He became the first African American Associate Justice on the U.S. Supreme Court.

Born: July 2, 1908
Died: January 24, 1993

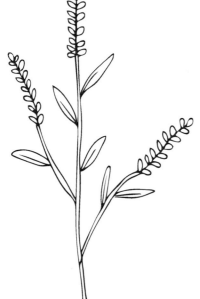

20

Sgt. William
Harvey Carney

"Boys, I only did my duty. The old
flag never touched the ground."

William Carney, who was born a slave,
became the first African American
soldier to be awarded the Medal of
Honor for his bravery during the
Battle of Fort Wagner in 1863.

Born: February 29, 1840
Died: December 9, 1908

Sean Moses' excitement was getting the best of him, so he decided to help his parents out.

"After I give you these clues, it won't be long before the lightbulb in your head turns on. Here are some facts about me: My name was Michael, originally. I'm known for my knowledge, and I graduated from Morehouse College. I also won the Nobel Peace Prize."

24

"Son," his father asked with a smile, "the man you speak of, did he have a dream? Did he March on Washington, and was his wife Coretta Scott King?"

25

On August 28, 1963, Martin Luther King Jr. gave his famous "I Have a Dream" speech at the Lincoln Memorial during the "March on Washington for Jobs and Freedom."

"Yes, Dad, yes! I'm Martin Luther, the king!"

"Martin Luther King Jr.," said his father.

"No! Martin Luther, the king."

"Martin Luther King Jr.," said his mother.

"No! Martin Luther, the king."

His father asked, "Okay, Sean Moses, what does that mean? What does it mean for you to be Martin Luther, the king?"

"Well, since I am going to be the king, I should probably wear a crown. I bet the one he wore was big, gold, and round. I can't wait for everyone to see! I'm going to be as great as Martin Luther, the king!"

29

"Martin Luther King Jr.," said his father.

"No! Martin Luther, the king."

"Martin Luther King Jr.," said his mother.

"No! Martin Luther, the king."

His mother asked, "What makes you think that Martin Luther King Jr. was actually a king?"

"Because his dream came true. Little Black kids can do the same things white kids do. And like Barack Obama, we can be President too!"

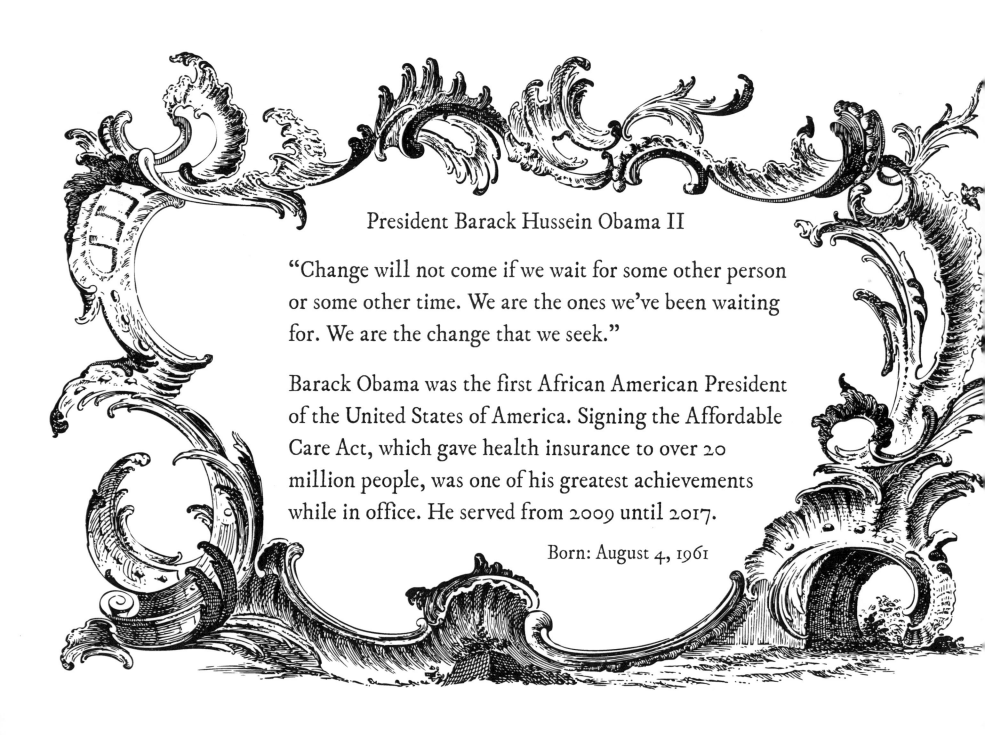

President Barack Hussein Obama II

"Change will not come if we wait for some other person or some other time. We are the ones we've been waiting for. We are the change that we seek."

Barack Obama was the first African American President of the United States of America. Signing the Affordable Care Act, which gave health insurance to over 20 million people, was one of his greatest achievements while in office. He served from 2009 until 2017.

Born: August 4, 1961

"That's why he's
Martin Luther, the king."

"Martin Luther King Jr.," said his father.

"No! Martin Luther, the king."

"Martin Luther King Jr.," said his mother.

"No! Martin Luther, the king."

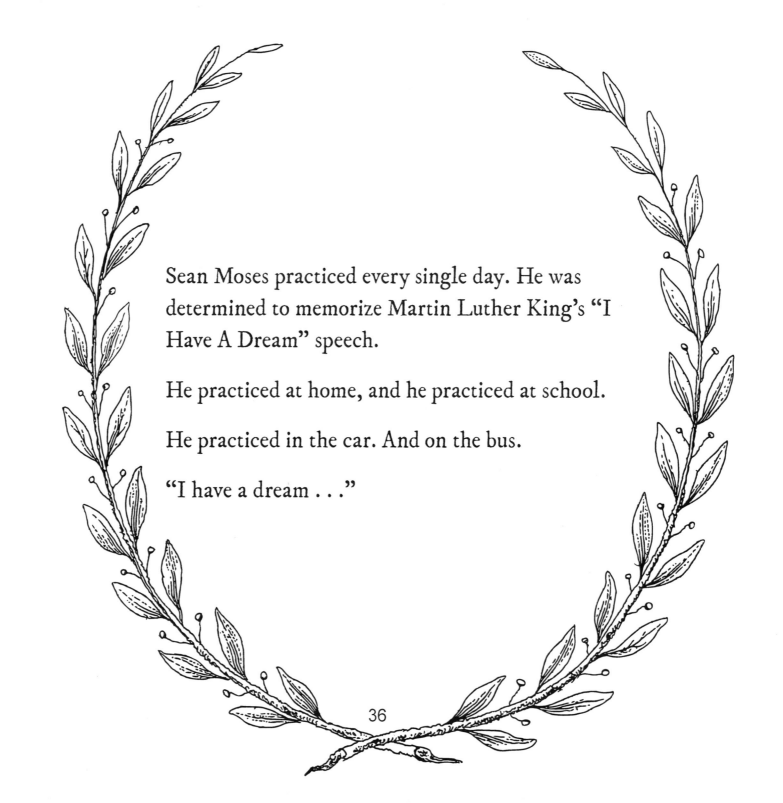

Sean Moses practiced every single day. He was determined to memorize Martin Luther King's "I Have A Dream" speech.

He practiced at home, and he practiced at school.

He practiced in the car. And on the bus.

"I have a dream . . ."

Sean Moses recited for his parents and some of his friends. He practiced again, again, and again. Until finally, it was time to perform.

Sean Moses walked onto the stage, clad in a robe of majesty.

A big gold crown adorned his head.

He stepped up to the microphone and boldly proclaimed . . .
"I AM MARTIN LUTHER, THE KING!"

The End

THROUGH THE YEARS:

Sean Moses as Dr. Martin Luther King Jr.

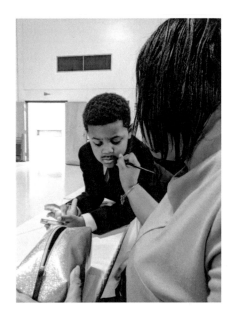

ABOUT THE AUTHOR

Moses D. Powe, MA, LCPC is the author of the children's picture book, *The One Book,* and CEO of POWEM Publishers LLC. Through this company he has built a robust platform aimed at helping fatherless fathers. As a Counselor, it has been his life's dream to provide quality encouragement along with the necessary tools to improve lives, motivate those in need, and offer a foundation for others to build on. He holds multiple degrees, from a Bachelor's in Psychology from Howard University to a Masters in Counseling Psychology from Argosy University. Born and raised in New Haven, Connecticut, Moses has lived all over the East Coast, including South Carolina, Washington D.C., and Maryland, where he eventually settled with his wife and son. To learn more about Moses and his inspiring work, you can follow him at www.mosespowe.com

ABOUT THE ILLUSTRATOR

Angelina Valieva was born into the family of artist Vladimir Valiev in Uzbekistan, and it was thanks to her father that she chose this fascinating profession. From a young age, her father directed her hand and taught her to draw. In 2005, she graduated from Republic Art College, where she studied graphic design. In addition to illustrating numerous children's books that have been published worldwide, Angelina has participated in various international art competitions and has won many awards. "Working with children's illustrations gives you the opportunity to go back to your childhood and feel like a child again. This is a fabulous world; there are no borders and nothing is impossible. It makes me really happy when I dive into the atmosphere of a fairy tale world again and again."

CPSIA information can be obtained
at www.ICGtesting.com
Printed in the USA
LVRC090035061221
705384LV00008B/145